FAITH OF A SALESMAN

Faith of a Salesman

by Harold H. Fletcher

Harold H. Fletcher

HERITAGE HOUSE

CHARLOTTE

FOREWORD

THE AUTHOR of this unusual book of poems is a traveling sales-man. He thinks of himself as a salesman despite the fact that he held pastorates for ten years in the Methodist church, and despite the fact that he continues to fill the pulpits of many different denominations as guest speaker.

To most traveling men the dull grind of traffic spells out tedium and fatigue. Harold Fletcher has learned to use the long hours of his lonely miles to commune with his Creator and to ponder the infinite reaches of beauty and truth. The soul of this traveling salesman has made for itself a habitation in realms of spiritual grandeur. The poems in this book are some of the songs which have welled up from the riches of his worship and meditation.

Since coming to High Point, North Carolina, several years ago, Harold Fletcher has been associated with the High Point Friends Meeting. He is a devoted member and worker, but he is interde-nominational in his thinking. In the Society of Friends he finds the freedom that his poetic mind and soul must have.

Quaker Men of the High Point Meeting discovered Harold Fletcher's rare ability as a writer, and insisted that they be allowed to sponsor the publication of a book of his poems. This volume is the result of their concern.

The poems in this book were not written for publication, but rather as spontaneous spiritual insights which clamored for expression. These poems are commended to the reader for their strength, for their depth of beauty, and for their richness of spiritual insight.

SETH B. HINSHAW
Executive Secretary
North Carolina Yearly Meeting of Friends

PREFACE

FROM its first appearance I have been angered by the popular interpretation of Arthur Miller's play, *Death of a Salesman*. The play itself, barring a few unrealistic areas, was a good play, and merited its reception. It had to have power to make such an impact. My criticism is not of Arthur Miller nor his play; I am vexed with the failure of the general public to see the purpose and meaning of Mr. Miller.

In the first place the play was written as a tragedy. To get a true picture of any facet of human endeavor tragedy as well as triumph should be portrayed. Each is realistic and has its place. We should be conscious of both.

Many people took *Death of a Salesman* as a norm for most salesmen rather than a picture of the exceptional. Certainly there are tragedies in the lives of salesmen the same as in any other occupational group; but my thesis is that the tragedy is individual and not occupational.

My hope is that some one of Arthur Miller's dimension will produce as powerful a picture of the other side of the question. There is romance, dignity, and triumph in the total story of salesmen. Only a small portion of the public is even faintly conscious of the indispensability of salesmen in the constant improvement of our living standards. Their story is a dramatic one, and they are truly "Knights of the Road." Their contributions and their triumphs are matter for a very large volume.

HAROLD H. FLETCHER

CONTENTS

APPLICATION

Every salesman knows that there are many ways of deception. All of us have
been tempted to rationalize it as not deception if the falsehood is only implied.

I had a session with my Lord,
We wrestled and He won;
And majesty came to the autumn sky
Before the day was done.
The clouds were lace in an azure dome,
And an all-pervading light
Suffused my soul and gave me peace
As day flowed on toward night.

The daily tasks of a salesman
Are sometimes fraught with snares,
And the devil leans on his shoulder
And leers while he shows his wares.
A question is asked with a dollar sign;
Temptation dangles the while
For the hidden lie in a cryptic word
And a truth-evading smile.

But like Hugo, the giant of massive thoughts,
I stand in perpetual awe
At the grandeur of an evening sky
And the sense of moral law.
The only legislation passed
That can solve the world's wide need
Is in congress of God with the wills of men
And a penitential creed.

TRAILWAYS

THIS is a travelling salesman's allegory. No more than men of any other vocation is he satisfied with the status quo. He is just as much a perfectionist and just as self-demanding.

The spell of dawn on a highland trail,
The smell of breeze and a waking bird,
And something whispers through the pines
Like a muted organ scarcely heard.
A symphony of multihue
That plays on pinnacle and spire—
And then the sun breaks through its bars,
And lo, the hills are all afire.
Then all of sense and mind stands still;
Nor does one strive for word or rhyme,
But quietly stands with his soul enthralled
On the rim of the world and the rim of time.

Then the road drops down to a sucking swamp
Where men are mired in its dark morass,
And you smell the stench of things long dead,
And the wheels clog down and the feet hold fast.
You moil and fight, and then you pray—
You reach good ground with breaking breath,
And your dull mind ponders in its pain
On high-tuned ecstacy and death.
You follow those roads, those awful roads,
Those wonderful, beautiful, dreadful roads—
You gain on the highroads a strength for the low,
And you somehow manage the heavy loads.

One can't regret when the trip is done,
For bad things fade and the good remain
As the good earth blooms when the storm blows out,
And you thank your God for the gift of rain.
When once you paused where the trailways cross
And chose by the pressure of circumstance,
You learn the art of journeying
And pick good footing at a glance.
Then the road turns back toward ecstacy,
And you pause for rest in a quiet cove;
And some power designs ineffably
That you meet with your quest in those you love.

CONFIDENCE

ALONE, yet not alone! A few years ago I had a letter from Badger Clark, the poet of the Black Hills. "I have spent twenty-five years alone in these beautiful hills, and the deserts of the southwest," he wrote. "Yet, I have never been alone."

I've pondered long this fellowship of years
With wind and trees and hills,
And all the raw, lone world apart from man,
Just as it left assembly lines of God.
Instinctively the souls of common men like me
Crave some retreat alone by night or day—
Alone, yet not alone—where we may find
That ancient and eternal values never change.
We crave some world blown clean of sophistry,
Of all pretense, and silly shams, and fads, and forms.
We love to see the earth washed clean by rain,
And catch the rhythm in the passion songs of storms.
We find in these the solidness of truth
Which all man's blind emotions can not change.
Obedience to law and loyalty to love
Will stand when armies fall;
And alchemies which God has put to work
Will yield abundance when our own economies have
        failed.
And so alone by night or day
We pause beside the road to pray,
And in a vale where falling leaves
Attest a planned fecundity
We find our faith and peace.

COMMUNION

FEW travelling salesmen would ever have taken up their profession if they could have foreseen the price of family separation. They really live from Friday night until Monday morning; selling is their way of paying expenses for the real thing. But some weeks when spring is bubbling they live all the time.

We'll have a happy time this week, my Lord,
And revel in the springtime's upward thrust.
We'll bypass erudite philosophers
And deal in simple thoughts like love and trust,
The common language of all humble hearts.

We'll not be burdened with the why and how—
Elusive to man's mind when at its best;
We'll race the winds across a living land
And quaff the hope effulgent in its breast,
Nor ever doubt the promises therein.

We'll let a week of dreaming run to dreams
While bloom and bower, and rain-washed sunbeams
        blend
Into the heartbeats of the fleeting hours
That fall in gentle dusk at journey's end,
Reducing all rapacities to peace.

And while we journey in the way, Dear Lord,
Let it not be an old Emmaus road;
Let me be conscious every singing hour
That thy hand lifts with mine upon the load,
And teach me how to share that joy with man.

ETERNAL NOW

TIME is the forge that moulds the experience and thought of a man into a comforting, if not completely satisfactory, pattern. After a day of ruminating between business calls and many miles of highway driving, I jotted down the following lines in the Prince Charles Hotel, Fayetteville, N. C.

Dear Lord, I thought to write a satire here tonight
To check my faith in fellow men, myself, and Thee.
I couldn't do it, Lord, if moon and stars should fall,
And fire and dust choke out the anguished breath of me.
Oblivion released the very fact of me—
I can't believe it has the power to draw me back:
Where nothingness lets go, Thy mighty hand takes hold:
Self-conscious mind escapes the cold organic pack.

It is primitive in logic, a concept of Thyself.
The whole of all existence fountainheads in Thee.
The hottest flame of all Mosaic utterance—
"I am"—is smelting truth to common men like me.
The birth pangs rise to jubilance—We Are! We Are!
It's not the things that were in time, or are to be—
Thou art!—the causal force in this *Eternal Now*—
The *now* that was, and is, and evermore shall be!

So faith in neighbors, blind impatience not with-
        standing,
Comes back like spring, and o'er their thresholds 'cross
        the street
I see the starting point of trails that blaze the world—
The sure impressions of their good, if stumbling, feet.
Then without struggle for a further claim to merit
I take my marching place in faith, nor ask to see—
I'll make my peace in compromise with all that matters,
Thou, Lord, *Eternal Now*, my fellow man, and me.

                                        Amen.

OMNIPRESENCE

THE day had started with strain, but the sales trip that had led me up and over Wagon Road Gap, and down past Looking Glass Falls ended in Shelby, N. C. that night. There the most natural thing in the world for me was to compose the following lines.

It's been so long since I've been orthodox.
I have no norms except the Spirit's breath
That touches all my world of sight and sound,
Gives gloom or grandeur to the daily round
In ratio to my own fidelity.

And when by God's good grace I stake my claim
Among the hills and streams of Paradise,
I want no golden pavements 'neath my feet,
No jasper walls along a shut-instreet.
Just turn me loose among the elements.

To live in fellowship with wind and sky,
To feel a rapture in the earth's deep clefts,
Hear silence where a roaring cascade falls,
Make answer when a lonely brother calls—
That's much of Heaven now, or afterwhile.

SYNTHETIC THRILLS

No mind is balanced unless it is willing to take truth wherever it finds it. Passing the cocktail bar in a fine restaurant I observed a large, artistic sign bearing this motto hanging over the mirror in the background:

> "Great minds discuss ideas;
> Average minds discuss events;
> Little minds discuss people."

Funny thing how men pay cash
For things to be got for nuthin';
They seek a thrill, a stolen sweet,
A fling at the dog or sumpthin'.
They guzzle down a handsome load
Of hifalutin' likker,
And hear the drums, and see the glow
Of lights that flow and flicker.
But give me the drum of a booming grouse
Where a wood copse sings to the wind,
And the low, dim lights of a rustic house
With a line of hills behind;
Or give me the color of gray and green
Where mosses grow on the stone,
And the splash of sunlight through the boughs,
And the fun to dream alone.

MEN AND MOUNTAINS

Two things inspired this theme: an old hymn learned from my mother when the only musical accompaniment was the voice of a summer night; and a couple of days on the Blue Ridge Parkway.

Dear Lord, I want to talk with Thee tonight:
Too much I've mumbled to myself alone:
Too oft man looks upon the rubble heap
Within his range of vision of Thy throne.
I saw the radiance of Thy form today—
A line of mountaintops against the sky,
Their slopes a torture to the climbing feet,
Their glades a glory to the distant eye.

I'm not afraid of saying the wrong thing
When talking, Lord, with Thee like this tonight,
For all the time I speak I'm hearing Thee;
I learn Thy mind and so get some things right.
Thy highland crests are only climbed with toil;
A blessing in Thy handiwork is pain;
Dimensions grow by strain, in flesh and soul,
Else all our fevered toilings would be vain.

And when at last I climbed the highest peak
On easy trails that other men hewed out,
I found a roaring glory in the sky:
The clouds boiled up in fury all about—
Out of the valley on the windward side,
Across the crown, to hang in veiling lace
Lest watchers on the levels far below
Should see, unearned, the beauty of Thy face.

In vast upheaval beauty rolled away
In rocky leagues man's feet have never trod:
The forests seemed to catch the wind and sing
A call to man—a litany to God.
And Father God, I've come back to the world
With wordless happiness within my heart.
An hour alone on Sinai with Thee—
What e'er Thou wilst I'll live my humble part.

And men and mountains, God, are much the same;
Each draws to each in strange affinity;

All men, like mountains, of unequal height
Are facile fragments of Divinity.
And Father of my soul, I give Thee thanks
That love and beauty know no altitude,
That night can fall and find Thee anywhere
To meet us in a tender parent mood.

WILL TO LIVE

LIFE is similar to a college track meet, except that in the race of life every
one who runs wins, if he is still running when the last whistle blows.

"In the morning sow your seed, and at evening withhold not your hand."
—Ecclesiastes 11:6

Life can't be based on a mileage score
That leads through many lands;
It is built by those who plant their feet
And grip it with their hands.

One might resent its austere rules
And Spartan discipline
Were it not for all the happiness
And fun that it has been.

There were times when the call of duty held
You tight like a tether chain,
And you whined to the call of the wanderlust
Like a pup with growing pain.

But you laughed a lot with the friends you made;
And your family came along:
You did your job and built your home
To the lilt of your secret song.

You met your scourge of punishments,
But these could never last
Once you made your itching feet dig in,
And made your hands hold fast.

You set your heart with your feet and hands,
And your structures slowly rose—
It's not so much what you got from life
As how you will make is close.

ASSURANCE

THE magnificence of the most ultramodern spot in which I had ever dined faded as if it had not been as I saw a clear sweep of the western sky. And that patch of sky had never changed in all the changes of man, and it didn't need changing. For four billion years it had been the same, and had never lost luster.

In that rich hour before the dark came down,
A western sky with cirrus clouds goldfringed
Splayed out the tale of man's immortal soul
With all its reach of hope with fear infringed,
Yet without proof of an ensuing dawn.

The mauves, and taupes, and golds toward darkness
    blended—
The grandest artistry I ever knew;
The ultimate of faith, and hope, and love
Flashed zenith-high—immutable and true—
And on the other end of night was day.

If a lone man could live his day pursuing
His Eden dreams, at night to have them end
In sullen darkness and eternal silence
With no sequence toward which his hope could bend,
It would not matter how depraved he ended.

But there is something in himself more certain
Than testimony of an evening sky—
The draw of soul to that vast Oversoul
In aspiration reaching far and high
To touch the fingers of a loving God.

PARADOXES

THE paradoxes of life and matter are most charming. Even the pain of wondering and questing is sweet. If life could be comprehended it would be too simple to waste one's time on. and nothing would have value. Only when we cease to wonder and to seek will life have lost its meaning. Our greatest logical certainty which can not be dethroned is that back of life and matter is a self-conscious Mind and Personality—we call it God and we can trust it. The one thing that insures Heaven against monotony is that eternity can never exhaust infinity, so we can keep on wondering.

Out of the loam mucky with rain
A lily grew—
Black into white like day out of night,
Spangled with dew.

Out of a youth savage for life
A faith burned clear—
Nurtured by tears—fruited through years
Ineffably dear.

Laws of a cosmos shaping in fire,
Divinely planned—
Order from chaos, beauty from pathos—
God's facile hand.

FUNDAMENTAL

THERE are docrines which take unity out of the universe, and then the universe loses its meaning. There is a kind of thinking that whirls on the pinpoint of a single science, and negates religion. Reality begins in the metaphysical and becomes concrete in the physical. The universe is a physical expression of metaphysical reality. Pinions, gears, wheels, carburetors, stylings — all are born in thoughts and ideas which are metaphysical, or above the physical, before they find concrete expression in automobiles. A tree or a television set, both express mind and personality.

> I want to get out, and away, and back—
> Out of the web of schemes,
> Away fromt distorted motives of men,
> And back to my honest dreams.
> I want to get back to the honest fields
> Where the wind can rip and wail;
> Where stars can blink their frozen light
> Through the blizzard's flowing veil.
> I want to be cold with an honest cold,
> Too honest for selfish deceit,
> And I can stand like a Nordic chief
> With the world beneath my feet.
>
> I want to be out where my heart can break
> Or shout its wild ecstacy,
> And the cry will blend into the storm
> In a symphonic fantasy;
> And my mind can soar without restraint
> In an infinite fellowship
> Which is never marred by a tolerant smile
> Nor the curl of a sneering lip—
> Where sophistry is melted down
> In a stinking scrap of pelf,
> And a lone soul's deep sincerity
> Is enough within itself.
>
> I want to read there in the singing night
> From a scroll of Holy Writ—
> Too Holy to be ever penned by man,
> Too vast for a manuscript.
> And there I'll find Christ in the frozen fields
> Swept by a midnight storm,

While I find Him not from the pedagogue
Nor his artifice, nor form.
And there I'll pray for earth-bound men
Who yearn for the verity
Borne in the harmony of wind,
And Christ, and the blizzard, and me.

OF MANY MEN

A MAN is next to God. A good man is a part of Divinity. This thought may violate the old orthodoxies, but the premise comes from the same source—the Holy Scriptures.

I recall him now. We differed some,
In ways that neither one could prove.
The moments were when tenseness reigned;
Our spirits grappled, both wills flexed;
And time distilled our mutual love.

I can't recall the differences,
Why each conceived the other odd;
I see his one lone silhouette
Against the total screen of life—
A good man, which is next to God.

—Tribute to Dr. Frederick R. Taylor.

PROMISE

MANY times I'd like to have said something like the following lines to some new-budding friend. But the finest things are hard to say well, and if real do not need saying. The friendship usually developed anyway.

Just a little bit of weather,
Bit of frost, and bit of dew,
Bit of wind, and bit of sunshine,
Bit of me, and bit of you;

Bit of starlight's velvet glances
Caromed from the sleepy bay
Where the ocean reaches inland
In a tired sort of way.

Something seems to feed the hunger
Of a spirit dark with care
'Till the burst of promise sweeps him
Into laughter unaware.

PHILOSOPHY OF A COMMON MAN

A MAN who works in a specialized field of science or mechanics needs watch himself lest he lose an overall perspective. A salesman, a social worker, a lawyer, a minister, or any other, should be no less alert to the same danger. An automobile mechanic would lose his spirit in his work if he didn't step back, now and then, and look over the new models in their complete and finished form.

Today I sweep aside my questioning of how,
I slight the thought of germ of minute molecule.
I want the sweep of wind on singing mountain peaks—
All lesser scopes I brashly flout and ridicule.
Nuclear fisson leaves a cold indifference—
Today I want no mechanisms torn apart;
I want the sight, and smell, and feel, and rip and roar
Of all exploding power of spring to fill my heart.

I want no gears or pinions scattered at my feet—
I want to see the finished structure of the whole.
An egomaniac who will not sell for less
Demands a universe as grazeland for his soul.
And so, I only tolerate the question "How?"
Until I get the answer to the question "Why?".
I think that God, like me, felt too much all alone
Until He made a world, a man, a tree, a sky.

Alone in secret place I talked with Him today:
The breaking pressures broke like waves on isles of peace.
I really heard Him on the hilltops in the wind:
The fading day, the glowing night brought full release.

SELF EXPRESSION

PERHAPS man is most in the image of God when driven by an irrepressible urge to express himself by mind or hand, or both. Perhaps self expression is as much a part of the nature of God as love, and perhaps that is *the why* of all creation—*the why* which philosophers have been searching for.

I think I understand, O God of mine,
How Thy pent-up emotions broke their bars,
And through the dark, abysmal skies of night
Flung out unending leagues of flaming stars.

I think I know the loneliness in Thee
Ensconced alone upon a throne of space,
Till from the urn of Thine own heart Thou poured
The fertile flow that made the human race.

That passion to express Thyself, O God,
To deck Thy skies with grand and fiery art,
Then make, and love, and bless such men as me,
Renews itself and burns within my heart.

MYSTICISM

A ROOM high in the Virginia Dare Hotel at Elizabeth City, overlooking the Pasquotank River where it widens out to meet the ocean, is a place where reveries and meditations come in rich abundance. It is a place to which you can come after your meanderings of the day, and have all your feelings crystallize into meaning.

Twining the arms of the ruby dusk
The jet trails foam then slowly fade;
And here I stand among old stones
Where a graveyard mourns on a hill's facade.

Jet trails, bones, and even names
Have lost their forms in the chemistry
Of a wild, grand thing I long have loved,
And I have no fear of its mystery.

The planes! The skies! The sunken sun!
The wind through the stones is not a knell.
When borne in the flight of these deathless wings
One finds the meaning of Heaven and Hell.

OLD MAN MISSOURI

THE following verses were written after an all-day and all-night vigil in the scenes they describe. A breaking tragedy had hit our lives and reason itself was fighting for balance. Fellowship with nature in the out-of-doors was the only arena in which a man could fight his battle, and find that his basic faith in his Creator could not be broken. The following poems, written under the same spiritual struggle, will be presented as conceived, without preface.

He marches through South Dakota
With his fine escort of hills,
Joins with the legions of sun and stars
For a rapture of beauty thrills.
Up from his placid bosom, seen from a crag on a far
    high rim,
His warm breath meets the morning chills
And rises to wreathe his rugged hills
In the very spirit of him.

He laughs when the midnight sprinkles
Its hot sparks in his eyes,
And he throws them back in a miles-long sweep
To the quietly playful skies.
And so the pageant glimmers on in soft infinitude,
And he stamps a pattern of the whole
On the lonely shape of a lone man's soul
In solemn quietude.

Deep in the marsh and rushes
Where you stand at his very side,
You hear the moan of a pathos borne
On the breadth of his restless tide.
You read the riffles of secret pain hidden beneath his
    breast,
And you ponder the fact of his proven might
And his own deep griefs beneath your sight
That will not let him rest.

You hear of his wild rages
From those who know him well,
When his anguish breaks in its overload
In a wild insensate spell.

But still they know his righteous dream and his
    unrelenting will,
As he pleads for constructive lift of hand
By intrepid men in a great wide land
His mission to fulfill.

Inexorably through the ages,
Through laughter, and beauty, and strife,
One cycle turns with its glories and pangs
Through all of the vistas of life;
Planets, continents, rivers, men—its turnings never cease—
Ineluctably it turns and then
Without lost motion turns again—
A flame, fulfillment, peace.

BROKEN WINGS

I got his message as his plane crashed down
Flashed through the ether of the miles of space,
That silent mystic call of soul to soul—
It came like tenderness of old goodbyes,
A poignant, swift reluctance without fear—
And I saw that later in his quiet face.

And what he felt in that last trice of time
Is not to me an awful mystery;
No fearful anguish marked his dizzy fall—
The peak of high adventure crowned his day—
No change of pace or courage as he went
To claim the sweetness of Eternity.

The call he sent to me was not a cry,
No desperation of a pleading prayer:
He knew the anguish that he'd leave behind
In dreams and plans unfinished with us here.
Instead, he thought, I'm sorry Moms and Dad—
Then met his Perfect Father waiting there.

SYMPATHY

A pall of desperation falls
As I grope in dark lights of a shabby street;
And I hopelessly love the wretched I see
For I know the drag of their wingless feet.

What guided me here at this midnight hour,
Or how far I came I have no ken;
But I see an expanse of the spangled sky—
I've a message of hope for my fellow men.

DUST OFF THE SUN

Dust off the sun and let its brilliance blaze again.
Too long you've threshed in frenzied throes of pain
'Til clouds of dry and fetid chaff have dimmed the light,
And only weird distortions of yourself remain.
Lift up your head. The far horizons still are there
Resplendent where the winter hilltops meet the sky.
A soft breeze rising from the southward stirs the air,
And promise, dormant for a season did not die.
Eternal indestructables remain the same,
And grand obsession still is cosmic, deep, and high.

Dust off the sun! Lift up the ceiling of your soul!
The blast that scarred your dream and bent your noblest
        plan
Rebuilds its damage in a stronger, tougher faith;
And early hope endures the flames that shape the man.
A seeming death and separation meets us all;
We all must walk, sometime, the long and lonely mile.
You didn't hear when law and truth first told you this:
A fleeting pain is mother of an infant's smile,
And thwarted dreams become the matrix of new hope.
Dust off the sun! Dust off the sun! And laugh the while.

INEVITABILITY

The ice, the gale, the torrents breaking—
You lean into the bleak, black night.
The selfsame winds, with all their aching,
Blow back again the kind starlight.

INDESTRUCTABILITY

I have found no place for a soul's rebirth like the
    gouged out crevices of earth,
And the lofty kinks of a mountain's spine in its ragged
    drape of rock and pine.
There you stand alone on the mountain crown—you
    can't see up and you can't see down,
For like the agonies of years in their blinding fog of
    futile tears,
A somber cloud bank folds you in, and the dripping
    silence becomes a din
As the breaking torrents lash and race through the
    stony seams of the mountain's face.
And yet, there works a paradox in this weird exile of
    tortured rocks:
A broken heart finds power to rise and fling new faith
    at the ripping skies;
The lightening sheathes his broken dart, the shadows
    melt and fall apart;
And in a vast bright world below, dashed with the gold
    of evening glow,
A vale of new-washed splendor gleams like the backward
    flow of your long-lost dreams:
Then you find that from the crux of pain your youth,
    refined, is born again.
Then there's the time on a lonely beach you yearn for
    the thing you can not reach,
When like the surge of some old grief the surf rolls in
    o'er the beaten reef;
And a tide comes in from the ancient years to engulf
    your mind in a thousand fears.
But the stars break out in the evening sky—Polaris still
    is riding high;
And something deep, and sure, and true, more than the
    cosmos wells in you—
The peace born of affinity with invulnerable Divinity.

YE CAN NOT JUDGE

There are vales where man must ever walk alone:
In moral choice no other of his kind
Can share the raging conflicts of his mind,
Nor weigh his heritage in blood and bone.

There's so much in the Truth of "Time in Flood,"
There's little in the height of man prefixed;
And only quirk of circumstance atwixt
The sludge of social dregs and royal blood.

THANKS AND VICTORY

Dear Lord, the years can't quite catch up with me
With Thy hand clinging to my own.
While flesh, and nerve, and bone, and brawn decay
The soul within has taller grown.

Thou hast led me in some agonizing ways
With thorny bramble overblown;
But never could a doubt blot out the faith
That where Thou led I'd find my own.

My grief and labor, common to all men,
Could never kill Thy given dream;
No night was ever dark enough to rob
The burning heavens of their gleam.

I've caught the years and hold them in my hand;
At my command they pay their fee:
My values dwarf the vagrant lure of gold—
They are safe eternally with Thee.

FROM WHENCE COMETH MY HELP?
Psalms 121

THE late bishop William A. Quayle of the Methodist church was once asked
under what conditions he had his greatest thoughts. In his own quaint way
he answered: "Alone, at night, in the woods, in a rain."

I knew a night of music not so long ago,
A valiant marshaling of every chord and strain
Played by the winds among the trees on distant peaks,
The crash of thunder and the rhythmic beat of rain.
Then changed the tempo of that swift symphonic
    movement:
The moon burned through the veiling clouds with
    subdued fire;
And mist and music filled the wild enchanted woodland—
A muted anthem that fulfilled my heart's desire.

I saw upon the sky at sunrise the bold stroke
Of artistry full careless of its drips and spills;
It fused its colors with the dewdrops and the streams
And spread its dreamy haze of glory through the hills.
I watched that canvas glow and grow through all its
    changes—
Unearthly genius flashing on 'til day had died—
A golden burst of passion in the stroke of sunset—
Then twilight—and my brimming soul was satisfied.

I see a multitude of lost and weary people,
God's children blinded in the fog of needless tears,
Rebellious, laboring, embittered in blind hatreds,
And tortured in the burning hell of baseless fears—
Needing only to look up and see the lighted glory
Aflooding down a summer woodland's pillared way
To galleries among the hills with all the music,
And all the paintings of the Master on display.

FAITH OR CREED?

MANY simply stated creeds, like goodwill and brotherhood, for instance, are universal. Many others are divisive and false, because they are based on arrogance, ignorance, prejudice, and provincialism.

No faith can still be faith when placidly
We take the dictums of a school or creed
And wrap them round ourselves in piety,
Content to meet a superficial need.

'Tis in the ugly buffeting of time,
In the lone vigils of the troubled mind
When desolate and bare the soul stands out
In bleak exposure to a freezing wind—

It is then that faith takes root and anchors deep
Against the fearful onslaughts of the storm,
And in unfathomed selfhood of a man
Takes its true shape in tried and rugged form.

There's no prescribing for the shape of faith;
Its surplice may be silk or tarnished clod;
For it becomes a tough, enduring thing
When man can pray, and laugh or weep with God.

REPRIEVE

To say "Thank you" in a way that conveys deep appreciation is the most difficult feat of language. We do not mean perfunctory thanks for the expected small things, but for those times when you are seriously at grips with life, and friends and neighbors show how good they are.

It's good to be alive, Lord,
And I thank you to the core.
It's great to share the working day
With friendly folk once more.

You've been lavish and indulgent,
Way you've shaped creation's plan;
But God, your heart was brimming
When you fashioned fellow man.

Just help me keep my face straight
When I meet the folks 'round town;
There's never words for feelings
That you have to keep choked down.

And God, on all my neighbors
Open up your precious store;
Whatever blessings they may have
Heap them up and give them more.

They have spells they're aggravating,
Just like me, but God, they're real.
Spite of all my lack of graces
Let them know the way I feel.

TO MOMS

MOTHER, Moms, Mabel, Midge—and many others—she has a myriad of names. She is hard to sneak up on, but we sure fooled her once, by getting her a sterling silver set two years ahead of her silver anniversary. It was a jolly surprise. In the top of the chest she found the following lines:

Would this could only hint how much I love you!
Your own pure, flawless luster through the years
Withstood all punishments, and heats, and pressures;
And took a polish dimming all your peers.
Whatever wear and grind abrazed the surface
You kept a solid color all way through;
And only sterling silver serves the purpose
To symbolize the quality in you.

And if at times my aging eyes are brimming
It's just the tender yearning of a soul
That fain would fold its shelt'ring walls around you,
And let all coming tempests break and roll.
And when on yonder flaming hills of heaven,
Or in the happy vales of Glory Land,
The Lord smooths down His garlands on your forehead
I still shall stand beside and hold your hand.

MIDGE

Skies ain't all been grey, my Darlin'—
Luminescence shinin' through—
More than mystic moon-rise charmin'
Every time I think of you.

Folks who never knew lone-lands—
Unobstructed night-time view—
Never knew the dawn abornin',
Never knew my love for you.

Folks who never knew the velvet
Of a dawn's fresh panoply
Ne'er could know the dewy sweetness
Of the love you have for me.

SPRING ABSENCE

AUSTERITY of circumstances once kept Midge and me apart for six months while I was setting up a new sales territory. The following is a letter I wrote her from the Carolina Hotel in Winston-Salem, N. C.

The city's distant din and drone are faint,
The far off purr of planes is almost mute;
But here the night wind in the pines is clear
As tones of reeds in some celestial flute.

From sunken rostrums in the teeming swamp
The chorus of the frogs is sweet and shrill—
The leader from his boggy podium
Plays with finesse upon his proudest trill.

Above, the sympathetic stars break out
And draw reflected laughter from the rills;
The modest moon peaks up and shyly smiles
Her mottled light across the wooded hills.

And irrepressibly the soil breathes
Her musky perfume at my fragile feet;
A bird, an insect chime in overtone
To make the charm of solitude complete.

Across a thousand miles, a million vales,
With spring's sublimity in fast repeat,
Above all cosmic volumes I can hear
Your whispered love ineffably sweet.

PARENTAL

WAR and Peace! It is still hard to be dogmatic about telepathy, yet some of use have experienced it. More than one parent has known to the day when a boy was coming home, or to the hour if he were never to come again.

The prow splits the waves which blend in a happy wake
Widening to fuse with a sunset on the sea;
Out of the west the boy is coming home,
And the Golden Gate swings wide, and glad, ajar.
The last of five long waits draws to an end.
The gulls soar high aloft, then dive again
Through claret dusk into the effulgent surf;
And hearts throb fast three thousand miles away.

At home, a thrush calls through the twilight hush—
The quiet trees stir with expectancy;
One set of footsteps never falls again—
Yet all the boys are laughing on the lawn.

OUR "IF"

NUMEROUS letters to our children have been written in verse. This was one, aping Kipling, written from a hotel room.

If you can probe the systems of the universe
From sprouting seed and sperm unto the outmost star,
Yet pause to quaff the glory of the whole ensemble
And know just how you fit the scheme for what you are;
If you can learn to tap the infinite for virtue
When weariness of flesh and mind draws shades of doubt,
And beat with bleeding hands upon eternal portals
And mock all odds of circumstance to hold you out;
If you can burnish all your tastes of mind and spirit,
And prize your growth in stature more than what you get;
If you can deal with gloom, and grief, and raw privation
And master all your own frustrations even yet;
If you can take the mystic fact of your own being
And find reality beyond a concrete goal,
And learn the grace of generosity in living,
You are the children of our very mind and soul.

—Mother and Dad.

THE LAST SENSE

WHEN one really believes in immortality, the thing we call death becomes only an episode in living.

> When all of Earth's beauties are dimming,
> And all of her melodies stilled,
> And the best of our dreams are ablooming
> With much of the fragrance we willed;
> The thing that will linger the longest
> In the wraiths of death's deepening mist,
> And keep our faith sweetest and strongest
> Are the voices of lips we have kissed.

AN ASPECT OF LIFE

A TRAVELING salesman is often an observer of grim aspects of life which have nothing to do with salesmen as such, and over which he has no immediate power to make better or worse.

The call of the earth is strong and sweet,
The pull of the flesh is sweet and strong;
But each must pulse to the magic beat,
In country field or city street,
Of the spirit's mystic song.

Life is a gift to be taken in whole,
There's nothing cheap in its fine brocade,
No meter breaks in its perfect scroll—
Even flesh is sacred when given a soul—
Of will plus God it's made.

But stop on a pantheistic note,
Or whirl on an instinct's savage breath,
And make response like a parrot's rote—
Then lyrics die in the strangled throat
And all in a man is death.

But look where the jubilant hills uprise,
With thumb on the page or hand on the plow;
And in seeing, see with more than eyes
The unseen of realities,
And you live in eternity now.

A PRAYER FOR OLD AGE

A COMMON fault is that we forget the old folks too soon. It is to men and women who have grown old victoriously that we owe our highest reverance and gratitude. Men who never knew it have gone with me on countless journeys and challenged me to something better in my native weaknesses. In their waning years they achieved their peak of greatness. Quoting Browning: " . . . the last of life for which the first was made."

Dear Lord, help me to grow old with grace like neighbor
    Bedfords.
I do not doubt the promise of Elysian bowers:
I only doubt myself lest life should lose its luster,
And waiting for the crossing as the sun goes down
My sense should lose the beauty of those twilight hours.

Help me to hold fast to my early boyhood wonderment,
Lost in the multihues of marvel everywhere;
Keep live my curiosity to delve and ponder
Perfections of Thy magic touch in earth and sky;
In stress let simple faith surmount all mundane care.

Help me to get and keep a rational perspective,
Some balance when impatient, migrant fancy calls;
Yet help me keep my visions of those younger years,
Redream those dreams from starry hilltops long ago
Until the last and momentary darkness falls.

Help me to be patient, Lord, with those of my own
    species.
Increase the pittance of my own poor power to give.
Teach me the art of sharing hope, and love, and laughter,
And sorrow with my neighbors on each other's doorsteps:
O God, until Thou callest me I want to live.

I thank Thee that the road to now has not been easy;
I've had enough of hurt to know another's grief.
That I might prize the splendor of the rugged highways,
And live with men asinging down our tears and fears,
Until I drop this shell of flesh—this is my brief.

AMEN

—To Nell and Clark Bedford

MUSIC

IN a pensive moment like that winter night in the Caldwell Hotel, Morganton,
N. C., long memories go back to deeper winters in the colder land of the
middle west.

The Gloria of cosmic sounds:
Those secret whispers close to ear
In soul-breath faith, "I love you, too"—
And baby sounds—and youth's career
In gaiety, and stomp, and shout—
Across the fields a neighbor's song—
And in the still of winter night
A sleighing chorus clear and strong;

And if to melody of voice
God strikes a harmony with these,
As harpist of the midnight hour
He strokes sweet music from the trees.

UP FROM THE EARTH, 1952

THERE are times when one momentarily draws a sharp perspective and sees himself as representative of many people who from their obscurity pushed upward from the bottom of a social order, were content to add their lifting power to the next generation, and then to be forgotten. The military salute to the achievements of the Wright brothers at Kitty Hawk produced this feeling.

The vast majority of people do make their contributions to an accumulating culture. We could not remember them all by name. A person has achieved a major victory when he accepts annonymity. In this regard Thomas Gray's *Elegy* is possibly the finest thing in all literature.

The frost is sharp in the furrowed loam tonight;
It also glints my uncombed, thinning hair.
My fingers tingle in the autumn soil
As I toy new sculptures from the promise there.
Why not? A jet armada boomed today
Rending in waves the sonic barrier
In skies above a shrine at Kitty Hawk,
Then dwined like summer thunder in the air.
Throughout the land politic voices ring
In mingled notes of doubt, and hope, and faith;
And some deep strength of spirit rises up
Across the land like morning's misty wraith.
In solemn mein more voices still are heard
Across the chancels in prophetic flood,
Exhorting men to sense of guilt and shame,
To sluff the vanities of greed and blood.
But sitting in my frosty furrow's curf
My crippled faith finds winged feet and runs;
I've vested flesh and soul in cosmic plans—
From here I raised and gave the world my sons.
Wherever thoughts, and deeds, and voices blend
Accumulated cultures slowly rise—
A motion sure but imperceptible
To earthy and impatient human eyes.
I know! I knew these fields a wilderness.
My mem'ry's much too long for luxury
To dull the knowledge of what can be done
When weeping people think, and work, and pray.
There's happy laughter, and there's singing, too.

God gave the world a boon in fun and song;
Then set to work a planned fertility
That crops of right could smother tares of wrong.
The flow of rightness did not dam and end
In noble patrons of the yesteryear;
Each generation has its quota new
Of stalwart souls to carry on from here.
I'm timeless 'neath these friendly stars tonight;
The frosty air seems, somehow, soft and warm;
My sons will cut a wider swath than I;
My world is sure, and built for any storm.

A COMPROMISE WITH TIME

No one takes time to believe it until they arrive, the falling years and the diminishing vitality. But it gives everyone, if he wills, a chance to become a genius—if he keeps his youth mentally. Time brings wisdom. Quoting Edgar Lee Masters: "Genius is wisdom and youth."

I have no quarrel with the falling years.
There is a path among the dewy bowers
Where God bestows fruition for our tears
And meters sunlight for our shadowed hours.

I see not why the coming years should dim
One's outlook toward the skyline far ahead;
I see His artistry, then thrust in Him;
I will not languish in a past that's dead.

To waken to the feel and sound of dawn
When drowsy recollection sweetly streams,
Renews a flagging faith long overdrawn;
And time selects and fills our choicest dreams.

Both God and years demand that dreamers dream,
Then bolster dreams with toil and sacrifice.
The broken hearts at end of Folly's gleam
Are those who sought to buy without a price.

I've figured my investments to a quid;
I'll ante up again while planets whirl;
I'll choose the wife and God whom first I did—
But I'm grand-dad of a giggling little girl!

A PRAYER OF WEARINESS

QUOTING Thackeray: "We are most of us very lonely in this world; you who have any who love you, cling to them and thank God."

Lord, give me while I need him most
A likewise needy brother,
That we may share in mutual prayer
The burdens of each other.

And silently while hands are clasped,
Above all mad turmoil
Help us to find in tranquil grace
The blessedness of toil.

Still all our wild impatience, Lord,
And each supporting each,
Help us to lift our eyes and see
Our dreams within our reach.

Refill our wearied spirits with
Such vibrancy of song,
That shared with Thee no load can be
Too heavy or too long.

Amen.

WHATISITALLABOUT?

My greatest friend often closed his conversations or his letters with: "I'm still wondering what it's all about." It was years in coming, that answer. The nurses were removing the oxygen tent. Everything—from a blade of grass to the most distant star—everything is about God and people.

I sang today along the way—
A lot of songs, the good old songs—
When life was young and hearts were gay—
And even in these somber years
Their leaping rhythms laughed in play.

I faced the prairie winds again,
Heard wild geese call across the night;
Forgot that ever life had pain;
And in a paean of delight
Stalked, face up, in a storm-blown rain.

I heard again the raucous shout
In hazy autumn afternoon,
When books were done and school was out,
And down our trap lines 'long the creek
We crept our stealthy ways about.

We'd read of Boone, Lewis and Clark.
And tried to pattern all their ways;
Built campfires in the early dark;
Spun yarns and fingered weapons 'til
Those fires burned to the last spark.

But best of all those melodies
Recalled young manhood's reaching ways;
More than all Heaven's parodies
A sweet girl's hairdo brushed my cheek,
And all the earth was rhapsodies.

Well, many years have flown since then;
I've sired a tribe, but without doubt
The richest thing within my ken
Next to my Christ—I wonder still—
That scented coiffure 'gainst my chin!

The wrinkles deepen, hair grows thin;
The falling years drape down their shroud;
But in all life's defeat and din
My song is raptured, strong and proud—
How tender, good, it all has been.

—To Jim Millen.

GREATNESS

THIS thought occurred while watching throngs in Springfield, Illinois and
again in Washington, D. C., and still again as I watched the labors of my
fellow parishioners in the building of our own House of Worship.

Monuments, hallowed shrines, memorials,
Volumes, canvasses and sculptured busts,
All formed from highest genius found in man
Immortalizing all that's best in man!
Through every land and nation of the earth
The throngs explore their shrines in hungry quest.
Response to greatness in itself is greatness,
Man's climbing toward the thing he'd like to be.
With all their Godward hungers undefined,
Graving the best of what is past in stone,
Who build or love these shrines themselves are great.

IGNORANCE

MAN only discovers the ways and systems of natural law, never how or why.
No exact science can originate or reproduce any equivalent of a single natural
law. Man has never really comprehended anything—not when you ponder
what the word comprehend really means.

How little one knows of the great wide skies,
Or the earth beneath his feet;
How little he knows of his brother men,
Of how, or why, or where, or when,
Or the boy and his dog in the street!

How little he knows of the tearing storms
And their power to blast or bless;
How little he knows of his own deep soul,
And the will of God to redeem the whole,
Or the depth of a child's distress!

NOSTALGIA

ONE never knows just what the stimulus is, nor where it comes from; but suddenly life, if bittersweet, is also delicious.

> "Who hath seend the wind? Neither you nor I;
> But when the trees bow down their heads
> The wind is passing by."—ROSSETTI

The senses sort out lovely things—
In summer dawns or autumn eves,
Some sweet, vague message in the smell
Of floating mist or rotting leaves,
Some color flashed from changing lights
That play new patterns on the skies,
Some feel or sound in wind or rain
Drips on the heart and dims the eyes.

They ring old music from the past,
And splash drab toil with mellow gleam—
Our minds still worship at the shrine
Of some ideal in some old dream.

TALKING WITH THE SEA

THE mind of a Druid or an Aztec should be no mystery to a modern mind. The chief difference between a pagan and a modern scholar is accumulated knowledge and increased enlightenment. Instinctively, now as then, one feels the Creator back of the thing created, and items of creation almost assume personality.

I know tonight the thing it is
Man always feels in kind with you.
Perhaps 'twas never said before,
Although it's stilled us o'er and o'er,
Forever ancient, always new.

Like man your great perimeter,
Your power beyond all comprehension,
Your depths that drop to mystery,
Your surface songs in wind or lea
Are only grasped in segmentation.

You sing, you roar, you laugh, you mourn;
You yield, resisting, some high call
That draws your very soul and mind
To judgments far beyond your kind—
You're all alone with God, that's all.

ANOTHER DIMENSION

IT has often been said that man stands between two eternities. It is just as true that he stands between two infinities. We can dwarf ourselves by always looking up and out without looking down and in.

I yearned toward the Moon with her flame in my eyes,
I spat from the pier to the froth of the sea—
Regardless of all their immeasurable reach
I was conscious of them while they never knew me.

I awoke to a bird, I smelled the perfume
Of rambler roses entrellised nearby
The sash of my window uplifted to Spring,
And the sole soul conscious to beauty was I.

So runs the refrain through all of the strain
Of cosmic convulsions toward system and plan:
The mass doesn't matter, nor distance, nor time
As much as the brain and the spirit of man.

ELEMENTAL

THE style of these verses are borrowed from Tennyson, but they develop a thought which I must express. Nights along the coastline do much for a man.

More than descriptive lines of rhyme
My soul would draw a deeper theme,
A thought far deeper than a dream,
The more I venture into time.

I face into the sea's wild spray,
Delighted in immensity,
Embrace the storm's wild tensity,
And stand enraptured while I pray.

The fleeting years roll on apace
Into the swell of eternity,
And in gloried stride with infinity
Suffuse my soul with higher grace.

Beyond the shrinking worth of pelf
Two truths surmount the wave or clod—
The all-pervading fact of God,
Responsibility of self.

INSPIRATION

THESE lines come from far out of the past when they were written. A young man in school, more than a year away from home, can learn one of the most valuable lessons in his education from the pangs of genuine homesickness.

An inspiration wafting in,
A hope comes all of Heaven-born;
A soul reads guidance from the stars,
And courage strains to meet the morn.

We thank Thee, Lord, that in the crux
Of all life's crucible and stress
No shadows fall but melt apart
Before Thy holy tenderness.

We thank Thee that no weakness comes
To rend Thy children part from part,
But flees before Thy purging light
When e'er Thy Spirit rules the heart.

We thank Thee that no barrier
Can rear itself against the scheme
Of him who in Thy Holy Place
Hath found the grace to toil and dream.

REFLECTION

SOME moments in life live forever. You are a very young man far from home, on a cold March night, after a hard day working timber. You are perplexed with the problems you meet when bridging from boyhood to manhood, and you have no counsel. You are insufferably homesick as you seek solace in your established habit of vigil with the night out of doors. There you can best find another Presence which is more than father, mother, and sweetheart. With Him, and with the muses you make out. Beauty seemed so indestructable.

> The cold wind moans among the barren boughs;
> The icy water gurgles on the bars;
> Still there remains some sweetness in it all,
> For in the shoals reflect a thousand stars.
>
> The tempter strives, and weakness is in me—
> Be it fate, or chance, or plan. I only bow
> And trust on Him whose likeness still I hold
> Reflected in my soul, I know not how.

SHOW US A SIGN
Matthew 16:1-4

Some, taunting, mocking, leering, said
"Show us a sign,"
When all the wealth of truth and proof
Shone dazzling bright before them
In a face benign.

Some, hoping, yearning, praying, said
"Show us a sign,"
When Christ had wrought infinite truth
With tender touch into
A clear design.

And still with clouded eyes we say
"Show us a sign,"
And while the milky ways swings 'round
We only see the night—
Our hearts repine.

With love and light brocaded into
Earth and skies,
In all the patterns, schemes and tones
That God could ply, we need
But lift our eyes.

QUESTIONS

It is not a lack of faith when one has to wrestle with cycles of temperament, or with pressure and strain of circumstances, and finds himself asking all sorts of questions. He stays on balance because he does have faith.

Why can't we take things just as they are—
October's gold maple, the glint of a star?
Why can't we settle for things commonplace
That thrall us in wonder like asters and lace?

Why can't one halt at the roar of a plane,
The rolling of thunder, a boy home again?
Why can't one slumber in arms sweet with love
As perfect in peace as the mourn of a dove?

Why must we penetrate eons of time
In blizzards of planets, in hoarfrost of rhyme?
Why can't we settle for one closest star,
Or the moon, or reflections from shoals on a bar?

Why can't we drift like the wind in the trees
When the world at midnight is on bended knees?
Why can't we stop at the burst of the sun
When all of the doubts of the long night are done?

Why should I struggle through one gloomy hour
With all of creation throbbing with power,
When God has decreed that I Am To Be,
And there's atoms of Him in a fragment like me?

OUR PASTOR'S REMUDA

THERE is a lot if good humor punctuating the seriousness of living. But humor is a serious thing, and should be taken seriously. It is a necessary ingredient in life, as a preservative and a shock absorber. Considerable truth is often packaged in the form of humor. But often a preacher's plight isn't funny.

Our pastor is in a handicap
Wrangling his flock through the afternoon;
And it's just too bad he can't cuss a bit
At the droopers who'd fail and flop too soon.

He tries to lead them where water is,
And herds them to browse on the finer grasses;
And he may know, or he may not know,
That some of his flock are just plain asses.

A flock or a herd, what matters the name?
He breathes the dust and the smelly air;
And his skin is red in the blazing heat
As he stretches leather to get somewhere.

But as he pushes for waterholes,
And drives for browse in the sheltered passes,
I wonder if it ain't silly of him
Not to check his herd for long-eared asses.

But a smatter of donkeys ain't such a mess;
There's some to be said for the dawgone fools.
If we can't be Arab steeds instead,
It's better donkeys than hybrid mules.

An ass is an awkward looking beast;
But here's a thought that I think immense:
In spite of his ears and his noxious voice
An ass may sometimes show horse sense.

I know my drover, and I can't get bad,
Though I flame the wrath of his sleekest steeds
As I snort, or bray, or run, or balk,
Or plain obstruct as may seem the needs.

How many are donkeys who bray all night
When the herd beds down as the day is done?
Count them over as best I can
I find that I am the only one.

And if it be in desert heat,
'Neath mid-day sun or midnight star,
My shaggy hide may spur the best
To thank their God for what they are.

MY FIRST POEM

I GOT in trouble with that first literary flourish, but it wasn't my fault. The janitor shouldn't have tin-canned that stray dog and then kicked him out on the highway. Naturally it inspired something, and when my note reached the end of that row of desks after I had passed it back, the high school principal was waiting there to confiscate it, and I got my ears eaten off. However, that principal was a hypocrite, for I discovered much later that my note had become a part of her scrap book.

Poor Doggie is very unhappy,
For Oh poor doggie is ill.
With a thing on his tail
As big as a pail
He ran yelping up the hill.